Divorce: How To Feel It, Live It, and Let Go

By M. SUSAN HAMILTON

THE FAMILY ECONOMIST, INC.

CONCORD, MASSACHUSETTS

Copyright ©1996 by M. Susan Hamilton
The Family Economist™
All rights reserved.
Published in Concord, Massachusetts
by The Family Economist, Inc.

Book design: FutureMedia, Chapel Hill, North Carolina
Cover: Dwayne Purper
Editors: Lisa Wynne and Joanne Kirk
Library of Congress Catalog Card Number: 96-96830
International Standard Book Number: 0-9653180-0-1
Printed in the United States of America

First printing: July 1996

10 9 8 7 6 5 4 3 2 1

INTRODUCTION

In the early stages of our separation, I digested more than thirty books, assembled my notes, and organized my ammunition. I was confident I had my divorce ducks in a row. In the early weeks, my ducks were scattered, and quickly filled with water. I was drowning. None of my reading prepared me for the bump and grind of the year of my divorce.

The psychological, sociological, physical, and emotional demands of getting through the day were more than the load-bearing walls of my heart could stand. I needed renewed inner strength and stamina to shore up my staying power. The days didn't get easier, they got harder.

If only I had located a 'divorce book' with some road signs, advance warnings, or maxims. Not a map, because every divorce route is different.

I needed some meditations, observations, and daily temperature readings on the fear, the pain, the anger, the disappointment, the hurt, the aloneness, and the emptiness that made my life so unbearable. In fits and spurts,

I kept a journal of my journey searching for inner strength. After writing more than 400 painful passages, I have kept a promise to my divorce attorney that I would indeed write a book if he would write the preface.

I hope and pray my unmarked route helps you along your divorce journey. Don't worry about staying completely on top of the water. You can swim. Keep trying. The stretches and strokes will get easier. You are worthy of the work. God bless.

M.S.H.
WEST SUSSEX, U.K.

DIVORCE: HOW TO FEEL IT, LIVE IT, AND LET GO

Dedicated in loving memory to my parents, Ruby Roberts Hamilton and W.W. Hamilton, and with love to my son.

With gratitude to my brother, James Sheridan Hamilton, the master of encouragement.

Preface

People dread divorce. It is a leap into the unknown. On one hand there is the personal trauma: the embarrassment of telling friends and co-workers; the heartbreak of watching your child see his world fall apart. On the other, there are the financial and legal complexities. A strange system of rules imposes itself upon the most personal decisions: how much money you must pay or receive, what property you keep, where your children will live and when you will see them. The most daunting aspect of the process is that as much as any occurrence in life, divorce involves change.

For the first time in years, a person will not wake up next to his mate. He will have to balance a checkbook and select mutual funds; he must go grocery shopping and cook his own meals; he will go to a party or family function alone. The change is all the more disruptive and disorienting because it occurs while the person is experiencing significant pain. In my 18 years as a divorce lawyer, I have seen countless people make the determination to end their marriage. It is a wrenching decision requiring at various times courage, selfishness, and faith. The process itself and its aftermath are generally faced with a healthy dose of rationalization. Like armor on the jousting knights of old, we protect ourselves with a selective historical perspective. We bury ourselves in work or a new romantic relationship or in the (sometimes overwhelming) details of the divorce itself. We do so because the pain might be too much to cope with if met with an open mind and heart.

A few of us, a rare few, have the courage to experience a marital breakup without blinders. Susan Hamilton has done this. This book is written from the perspective of a woman whose marriage is dissolving after 21 years. Susan faces this without rancor, blame, or self-aggrandizement. Aside from being one of the best-prepared and most meticulous clients I have encountered, Susan has the soul of an artist. Her insights go to the essence of divorce: its tragedy, its absurdity, its humor and, ultimately, its power of redemption. As painful as the divorce process can be, it is also a rebirth.

There are few times in life when one can wipe the slate clean and begin anew. Susan appreciates and describes the roller coaster that is a dissolution of marriage. The reader will find the journey a little less bewildering after reading this book. More than that, this work shows that at the end of a long, difficult trek, there will be days when the sun shines, a warm breeze blows, and peace fills the heart.

WAYNE D. EFFRON,
ATTORNEY AT LAW
GREENWICH, CONNECTICUT

Cross-pollination during marriage is called an AFFAIR. CROSS-EXAMINATION in Divorce Court is called DISASTER. A CROSS-TEMPER after divorce is called WITS' END.

After that, it's called BEARING THE CROSS.

The tongue's not steel, yet it cuts.

Divorce is a SINGULAR EXPERIENCE. DEFINITION OF SINGULAR: A composed word. A divorced person becoming SING-le after attack to the jug-ULAR.

One is not so soon healed as hurt.

During divorce, nothing else in life matters. It is survival of the fittest, but I forgot to sign up for a Cross-Training Course. My EX is a tri-athlete with three skills:

My Way, My Way, My Way.

I will give up trying to understand my EX. It is an exhausting exercise without benefits.

We must not look for a golden life in an iron age.

If I strive for truth and justice, I shouldn't go through divorce. Truth, justice, and fairness were deleted in the recent volumes of Marital Law. Neither the lawyers nor the judges felt they were statutes of primary importance in today's marriages.

Divorce is not fair. Life is not fair. The earlier I give up searching for fairness, the earlier I can make a life.

...Who am I, O Lord God, and what is my house, that thou hast brought me thus far? **II Samuel 7:18**

Is divorce a dysfunctional dynamic I was born with, growing and dividing in my cells until it consumed my heart and brain? Something like being born and registered a pitbull puppy:

"Divorcée-in-training."

A wise man changes his mind; a fool never.

Tryst is not an ancient spelling of modern trust.

There is nothing more desirable than a free mind.

DIVORCE: HOW TO FEEL IT, LIVE IT, AND LET GO

Divorce is White-Knuckle Flying. At least in regular life, I picked my own departure and arrival schedules.

The higher the ape goes, the more he shows his tail.

"Over-Drawn Lifers" didn't affect me. My life was simple.

I just wanted a marriage that wasn't burned out or even charred around the edges. Instead, my life went up in smoke and vanished before I located the source of the fire.

He that's afraid of leaves must not come in a wood.

Our son's back-to-school gift this year was his father's leaving home. How do I instill trust when his own flesh and blood is teaching Basic Betrayal 101, a noncredit life course?

In those days there was no king in Israel; every man did what was right in his own eyes. **Judges 21:25**

Kids don't start fires with matches they don't have. Divorces don't strike marriages with affairs they don't have.

The web of our life is of that mingled yarn, good and ill together.
All's Well That Ends Well

I need Divorce Day Care. I could drop in for care and guidance through eight to ten hours of the long, dreaded days of divorce.

Or maybe I need Divorce Night Care. Mostly the nights are the worst.

Let never day nor night unhallow'd pass,
But still remember what the Lord hath done.
Henry VI, Part II

September 12

There are three basic DIVORCE PHILOSOPHIES:

I. "PLAY-IT-BY-EAR" DIVORCE
Listen to opinions, gossip, and advice from family and friends.

II. "BY THE BOOK" DIVORCE
Read all the books, articles, and support literature available. Take my attorney's advice as the Holy Grail.

III. "INTUITIVE PERSONAL PLAN"
Each day I listen to my own intuitive voice. Pray fervently. Believe in myself. Read the divorce books. Develop my own personal life plan. Exercise and feed my mind. Exercise and feed my body. Ride the waves of self-motivation and confidence. Divorce, too, will pass.

Gossips and frogs drink and talk.

THE SWALLOW AND THE DORMOUSE
A Fable

A swallow, while the year grew old
Ere yet was felt the winter's cold,
Chanced in a meadow to alight,
And as he plumed his wings for flight,
A dormouse slowly past him bore
A load to swell his tiny store,
"Is this a life," the swallow said,
"By conscious beings to be led?
I, when the days grow chill and brief,
And age embrowns the shrinking leaf,
Borne on fleet pinions, gladly fly
To bask beneath a gracious sky,
That smiles in winter as in spring,
Nor numbs with cold my soaring wing.

You have a refuge from the air,
But what is your enjoyment there?
Coiled up within a dusty heap,
Not even to feel, in that dull sleep,
The warmth and peace so dearly prized —
Call you this life? 'tis death disguised."
The dormouse mildly answered, "True:
I seek not to compare with you;
Blest are such ever-genial days;
Yet, ere you blame my quiet ways,
And boast what pleasure travelling brings,
Remember this – *I have no wings.*
To keep chill winter from my door,
I do my best – what can I more?
For bliss like yours I ne'er was meant;
Seek not to rob me of content!"

PICA

In a thousand pounds of law there's not an ounce of love.

Scientists are constantly refining methods for air-traffic control and birth control. Why not work on divorce control? We need help keeping aflight the unborn divorces.

Happy are they that hear their own detractions, and can put them to mending.
Much Ado About Nothing

What motivates the divorce motor? It spits and sputters, the red warning light goes on, and then it's too late for road-side service. Life is a dead stop.

If I had faithfully done regular service maintenance, would I have recognized the problems earlier? Matters not, I got traded for a later model.

A man without reason is a beast in season.

Whe I read my office mail I have to read it over and over again to clear my head enough to reply. I cannot think. I am afraid to think. Afraid to make decisions now. God, just get me through this hour of decision.

...O Lord, there is none like thee to help, between the mighty and the weak. Help us, O Lord God, for we rely on thee, and in thy name we have come against this multitude... **II Chronicles 14:11**

Surgical Siamese twin separations are less complicated than divorce. The surgeries also have a higher survival rate. Divorce requires greater faith than surgery, and the healing is often drawn out beyond original expectations.

No lock will hold against the power of gold.

I am trying to teach our son a moral and ethical code of behavior. Then the playground teaches universal values and a decoding process.

When adulthood is finally reached, what goes wrong? Are the playground bullies now divorce bullies? Are the silent and swift now divorce-fluent? What behaviors go awry? Why couldn't I identify a divorce candidate? The playground was never fair at any age.

Have but few friends, though many acquaintances.

What do I do with my used wedding ring? Do I melt it down and make pierced earrings to symbolize my pierced heart? Perhaps I should melt both of our rings together and save the gold for our son's wedding ring? Why would I want to give him tainted gold?

In time of prosperity, friends will be plenty,
In time of adversity, not one amongst twenty.

Maintaining my energy is a tough challenge. The mental drain taps out my physical reservoir.

If solar energy, electrical current from waterfalls, the heart pump, and rechargeable batteries carry on for unknown spans, surely I can gear up enough energy to get through this day.

Spiritual energy is without measure or limits of time.

Foxes, when they cannot reach the grapes, say they are not ripe.

There are few pinnacles of pleasure while going through divorce. High on the short list might be a hot bath. Higher still might be a completed divorce in less than 12 months.

After that, the real tough negotiations begin.

He loseth his thanks who promiseth and delayeth.

Rapid-firing emotional cannons are attacking most people in my immediate range. I cannot get a grip today.

In my distress I called upon the Lord; to my God I called. From his temple he heard my voice, and my cry came to his ears. **II Samuel 22:7**

Little negative statements, small negative events, minor negative thoughts become the brush fire that takes down my house.

I'll stay on the positive thought train to railroad Divorce Depression. Nothing is powerful enough to bring me down. I'll try to be with positive people.

Good bees never turn to drones.

Curious about my daily Horror-Scope?

Call my divorce attorney or mediator. He or she will give you my daily forecast and lifelong prospects without consulting my chart.

The nightingale, if she could sing by day,
When every goose is cackling, would be thought
No better a musician than the wren.

Merchant of Venice

Divorce scholarships are not commonly available. I cannot depend on anyone for financing.

Divorce is my call to higher learning. I can finance it over time or cash out my problems immediately.

Have more than thou showest,
Speak less than thou knowest,
Lend less than thou owest.

Lear

Does divorce mean that one is Dollar-Poor, Off-The-Mark, Pound-Free, Un-Yen'd and Franc'd-Out? Maybe universally it means cash-less and applying for credit.

You came for wool, but shall return shorn yourself.

If a divorcing couple were on a deserted island surrounded by salt water, only the one who owned the gun would eat.

Do not be afraid of sudden panic, or of the ruin of the wicked, when it comes; for the Lord will be your confidence and will keep your foot from being caught.
Proverbs 3:25-26

I can probably pick from eight generations of matrimonial lawyers who have built divorce camps in this country. Of all the available lawyers, I knew the second attorney I interviewed was mine.

Unlike some divorce lawyers who like to circle the wagons, build a flashy bonfire, and roast a lifetime of food on one fire, mine was different. Mine dispatched some well-oiled wagons, built a respectable fire, but made certain my son and I would have food.

Scald not your lips in another man's pottage.

Divorce is not the time to feel around in the dark for information. I need to vigorously search for every receipt, record, bill, invoice, and document that will substantiate my case.

I am my attorney's private investigator and super-sleuth. He or she can only build my case based on the segments of information I supply. Divorce is self-service.

Calmness is an art. Silence is a science.

Heigh-ho, heigh-ho, here we go!

Another clear day spent in the divorce dungeon deciphering divorce documents. How do I become divorce-fluent for life? Who would want to be?

You stout and I stout, who shall carry the dirt out?

Divorce problems are a NAG DISK that enters my computer. The information is hard to retrieve, refuses to stay filed, and always produces a smeared printout.

My reasons are most strong, and you shall know them.
All's Well That Ends Well

Divorce is discovery, drudgery, dead-end chases, and dismal dog meat. If I don't do the paperwork, I won't even get the scraps.

Opinion's but a fool that makes us scan
The outward habit by the inward man.
Pericles

Smooth divorce documents are like folding fitted sheets. I pick and choose the places to hide the wrinkles and imperfections. Maybe it all gets ironed out over time.

...do not be anxious beforehand what you are to say; but say whatever is given you in that hour, for it is not you who speak, but the Holy Spirit. **Mark 13:11**

Divorce negotiations are like a giant Swap Meet. I have already stepped in dog dung on the way to my bargaining booth, reinforcing: LIFE STINKS. My attorney and I are in a rented open booth. We are exposed to sizzling sun. The swirling dust clings to my sweat.

My EX just slipped out of his attorney's limo into an air-conditioned Persian-rugged tent, hiding behind closed flaps. My EX is calm, cool, and fully imbibing his first celebratory drink. The negotiations haven't begun, but his attorney assured him: The swap meet is O-V-E-R. Now revise this scene. I'll visualize I'm in control. My attorney is the Kingpin and I'm Queen of the Tent.

When a dog is drowning, every one offers him water.

W hat was so bad about our marriage that we had to get divorced?

In nature there's no blemish but the mind,
None can be called deform'd but the unkind.
Twelfth Night

Divorce problems resemble dozens of loose eggs without cartons. They're too fragile to move. Traveling for help is out of the question. The rooster has disowned me. The chances of getting to the market with the eggs intact are slim. What to do? Sit and rot?

I will try to deal with the problems (and eggs), one by one. I will give them my complete attention or they'll break. I will move quickly. They eventually will rot, if unattended.

The lion's skin is never cheap.

For some people, divorce is a volcano that covers their world with hot, burning lava, leaving lifetime scars. For others, it is merely a lava lamp, easily unplugged, trashed, and replaced with a stronger, truer light.

Events in my life are only as large as the space I allot them, the time I allow, and the mental image I carry forward.

Our bodies are our gardens, to which our wills are gardeners. **Othello**

Divorce is like a massive bee sting. I know it's going to hurt, but I can't run fast enough to avoid getting stung. When it actually happens I realize I forgot how much pain really hurts.

He who withholds kindness from a friend forsakes the fear of the Almighty.

Job 6:14

What is the total cost of my divorce?

How many years of brain bruising?

How long will I feel social-clotting that keeps me from circulating?

How many muscle spasms in my chest?

How many millimeters of heart plaque?

How many extra pounds of fat frustration?

What kind of career compromises must I make to juggle my new family structure?

How many argued dollars?

The Golden Age never was the present era.

Not a day goes by that I don't doubt whether I should have waited until our son finished college before I divorced. Would it have been better, bearable, then?

Good deeds remain, all things else perish.

If crying is cleansing, my body is flushed out daily. Why do I put the toxic thoughts back on the CD player in my brain? I play the divorce tunes over and over ad nauseam.

I am trying the Purity of Silence for two minutes today. Prayer. Silence. Prayer.

Every day brings a new light.

My eyes are always red, even when I'm not crying. My eyes hurt. The hurt behind my eyes is divorce pain. None of the medicines available can even touch the edge of this pain.

Repent what's past, avoid what is to come,
And do not spread the compost on the weeds
to make them ranker.   **Hamlet**

Divorce takes place in a democracy. What transpires behind closed doors has nothing to do with the democratic process.

What happens with divorcing couples in public is violent-mouth syndrome, not freedom of speech. By mail, coerced signatures are sent on dictator documents. Divorce is not even close to a democratic process.

He that eats the king's goose shall be choked with the feathers.

It required advance planning to live through each of the holidays within our new family structure.

The first Thanksgiving, my EX promised to come to our house for dinner, for our immediate family. A week before, he said, "I've decided I don't want to come." Our son was stunned.

First, I was hurt, then angry, and then enraged that I could still be hurt so easily. I finally realized I had to begin our own new holiday traditions for my son and me. If we invited our extended family, our neighbors, and others truly in need, it would be our way, our tradition. We are re-building our life our way, filling our souls once again.

He loseth nothing who keeps God for his friend.

What is the currency for divorce dollars? I understand the daily rate varies according to the Dispositional Mood Traders.

Right now, my resources are depleted. I need outside traders to bolster my market share and futures. Call me when my market plan goes up. Now, I am experiencing enough of the down side.

Hope is a good breakfast, but a bad supper.

Divorce is disempowerment of my entire universe. Post-divorce empowerment is establishing order in my remaining world. Something like having enough money left to go out for breakfast.

...and if the Almighty is your gold, and your precious silver; then you will delight yourself in the Almighty, and lift up your face to God... **Job 22: 25-26**

If naming a product is key match point, you don't want to use the word divorce.

"DANDY DIVORCE CARAMEL CHEWIES" doesn't get it. Nothing about divorce is dandy or sweet.

Every slip is not a fall.

Various cultures have hung meat to cure and left salted fish out to sun dry. What do they recommend to preserve divorced and broken hearts?

The ripest fruit is at its peak a brief moment.
The seasons in life are short.
I will enjoy the growing periods, too.

Divorce denial is part of the beginning, middle, and end of this year. Divorce dew uncontrollably dampens my pillow each night.

...for the Lord searches all hearts, and understands every plan and thought.
I Chronicles 28:9

HOW TO GET A HOUSE OUT OF AN EMPTY BARREL

Put the barrel into a secure place, near a spring of good water, on the road to the grog shop. When you want a drink, take the price of it in your hand, and start to the grog shop – go as far as the spring, drop the money into the bunghole, take a good drink of water, and return home. Repeat this operation til the barrel is full; knock out the head, and you have the price of a splendid brick building. Fact.

English, c. 1857

Would you thatch your house with pancakes?   **English**

How do I give a three-sentence answer to: "Why are you getting divorced?" In future years, will it be a two-sentence answer? Maybe I'll know the reasons then.

A woman's thought runs before her actions.   **As You Like It**

In divorce, like surgery, you see a lot of blood and guts before closure. In time, the wound sometimes heals or temperamentally becomes inflamed.

Healing is a personal, inside job. The surgeon, the attorney, the mediator, and the judge all walk away.

Once again, I AM ALONE.

The thunderbolt hath but its clap.

My couple friends want to take me out to dinner. I don't want to go...ever. If I went, the tables would be for 3, or 5, or 7 people. If I went, what would I talk about? They are always so light-hearted. My heart is so heavy now...my body can barely lift it to walk, let alone laugh.

Wise and good is better than rich and great.

THE GOURD AND THE PALM

A gourd wound itself around a lofty palm, and in a few weeks climbed up to its very top. "How old may'st thou be?" asked the new comer, "About a hundred years," was the answer. "A hundred years and no taller! Only look, I have grown as tall as you in fewer days than you count years." "I know that well," replied the palm, "every summer of my life a gourd has climbed up round me, as proud as thou art, and as short-lived as thou wilt be."

There is no pot so ugly that a cover can be found for it.

When I gained weight in pregnancy, I thought of *what will be*.

When I gained weight in divorce, I thought of what *might have been*.

Who will not keep a penny, shall never have many.

In marital therapy, my EX mentioned he hated my lipstick. I asked him what color he would prefer, but he couldn't be specific. He could only reply, "Just something different, anything other than what you always wear."

Strange, because I wear three or four different colors in any given week. I wonder which color he hates. Is that why we're getting divorced?

Courage mounteth with occasion. **King John**

I feel utterly, completely, totally overwhelmed. I have fifty things to accomplish today and no sense of priority. I have a pen in my hand and an empty page before me, but I do not know what to write.

Should I write down all fifty things and try to make sense of it?

Should I do two things today? Maybe one?

How poor are they that have not patience. **Othello**

Divorce anger is deadly. It can turn ordinary drinking water into bad blood. It diverts my hunger and makes me eat irregularly. Anger sours my digestive juices. It is a constant interruption in my sleep patterns. Anger contaminates my brain circuits to produce Short Temper Syndrome. It keeps my daily pace stuck in the same gear: slow.

The Lord is my shepherd,
I shall not want;
He makes me lie down in green pastures.
He leads me beside still waters;
He restores my soul.
Psalm 23: 1-2

When our son was four, a family friend gave him a hand-painted sixteen-inch Santa Claus. She sanded it, painted it, and installed a music box in the back. When my son twists Santa's big red nose, it plays, "Here Comes Santa Claus."

We have treasured hand-knitted stockings, handmade ornaments and hand-crafted candlesticks, but our son's Santa is beside the crèche. Little traditions are big memories before and after divorce.

But he who does what is true comes to the light, that it may be clearly seen that his deeds have been wrought in God.   **John 3:21**

My son has an expression: "I'll give you five seconds to lose it." It means, "Mom, I've got the picture. Go on to the next subject. Don't drill me to death."

In divorce, I can't seem to remove the drill on a subject. It grinds harder, louder, and more shrill until my head pounds in pain.

I will give up the drilling method. It doesn't work for my life and the people around me. It is hurtful. Divorce drills and burns.

To a crazy ship all winds are contrary.

I can't even imagine the first Christmas alone when my son is away with his Dad.

And if you will hearken to all that I command you, and walk in my ways, and do what is right in my eyes by keeping my statutes and my commandments. ... I will be with you, and will build you a sure house ... **I Kings 11: 38**

Son: "You're just a mom; I don't have a family anymore."

It is a mistake to look too far ahead. Only one link in the chain of destiny can be handled at a time. **Churchill**

I am not Momdad. I am not Motherfather. I am neither a bridge between two continents nor a flash of lightning between two trees. I am only the lifetime mother of my child; the mom of his young life. I am giving motherhood my best shot because I will not be given another chance to live this day with my son. Our individual lives are only the sum total of all the separate days.

No person was ever honored for what he received. Honor has been rewarded for what he gave. **Calvin Coolidge**

I feel distraught. Or maybe I was DIS-TAUGHT. Am I divorcing because I didn't learn life's lessons during childhood? Or didn't my parents get it right? Right or wrong, they were married fifty-two years.

It is not easy to straighten in the oak the crook that grew in the sapling. **Gaelic**

Divorce anger is one of the most stubborn stains to remove from life's fabric. Some days, I wear the stains front and center. Other weeks and months, I can eventually work on the anger until it is released forever.

It is never too late to mend.

Anger is an hourly and daily job. Screaming in the basement helps. Releasing anger from my body is possible and wholly necessary to make space for new happiness. I will learn to breathe deeply, drawing in clean air on a slow count of ten. I will slowly exhale the ugly anger out on a count of ten. It is a lifetime skill worth daily practice.

It is good to have two strings to one's bow.

I don't have any sense of order. I can't even separate the days from the nights. I am sleepy all day at work and fitfully awake at night.

I will work on this problem one night at a time. Just give me a few days to think about it.

When the sea is calm, all boats alike show mastership in floating.   **Coriolanus**

I've finally accepted that divorce is an unexplainable physical, psychological, environmental, sociological, circumstantial state that is not forever. It just feels like forever.

Every couple is not a pair.

Anyone who says they had an easy divorce can also cut a mango into perfect slices. They are both deceitful and impossible.

For I am sure that neither death, nor life, nor angels, nor principalities, nor things present, nor things to come, nor powers, nor height, nor depth, nor anything else in all creation, will be able to separate us from the love of God... **Romans 8:38-39**

Why do my days run together? I can't seem to reach higher ground to gain perspective. My heart races all day. My legs feel like lead posts. I'm not sure each step I take is forward.

Eaten bread is soon forgotten.

Divorce isn't for runners, or for those who walk. Divorce is a rented walker with a dead-weight body dragging herself to an unmarked finish line.

When like the bees, toiling from every flower,
Our thighs pack'd with wax, our mouths with honey,
We bring it to the hive. **Henry IV, Part II**

Divorce is an annoying dripping faucet. Quickly it turns into white water rafting, only I don't remember slipping into the raft. There wasn't time to clip on a life saving vest.

The roaring screams are deafening. Some days, I'm sure I'll die.

He that will have a cake out of the wheat must tarry the grinding.
Troilus and Cressida

I used to go crazy if I found a dog hair on a dinner plate. Divorce is beyond dog hair.

An ape's an ape, a varlet's a varlet, though they be clad in silk or scarlet.

Why do I lie when people say, "How are you?"

"Oh, fine. I'm just fine."

I'm not fine. Every day, I'm dragging my body to work with a hemorrhaging heart.

My heart barely has the pulse to pump anymore. My heart is broken, aching, open, with no immediate help in sight.

Maybe I'll call 911. What should I say?

A quiet tongue shows a wise head.

Son: "Mom, why don't you laugh anymore? You're always so serious. Don't you want to have fun anymore?"

He that wants money, means, and content, is without three good friends.
As You Like It

How can I change my DNA?

DNA: DIVORCING NEGATIVE ANGER

I was not born with a negative imprint, and I will not die with it. In the meantime, I want to diminish its power in my cells, bossing my body. I am the boss of me. I, alone, with God.

When a thing is done, advice comes too late.

There is a hushed, profound sadness in divorce. It is easily read on the faces of the children. It is carried in the hearts of the parents.

'tis in ourselves that we are thus, or thus. **Othello**

I feel an emotional numbness in divorce. The pain can't be this bad. My fingers are numb, and they won't hold the pen steady enough to write the final words on these legal documents.

Is brain numbness an inability to act? Will I be numb-struck like this forever?

A penny-weight of love is worth a pound of law.

If divorce sucks out life, what is my source of nourishment?

Honor the Lord with your substance and with the first fruits of all your produce;
then your barns will be filled with plenty, and your vats will be bursting with wine.
Proverbs 3: 9-10

While my car is pulled through the car wash, I want my brain washed. I could do with a complete hosing out of this year's grit and emotions.

He that blows in the dust, fills his own eyes.

In the constellation of life, are the married planets upscale and the divorced planets downscale?

What kind of meteor dodging do I have to do to get equal lighting by day?

By night, the evasive planet shadows are all treated the same.

A good conscience needs never sneak.

I don't have a spare minute. I don't have time to cry at work. At home, I need to organize the divorce papers for my attorney meetings. I need to find twenty minutes for a good crying cleanout.

It is easy to bowl down hill.

It is a lawyer, a mediator, and a stranger asking me to order from a menu while I am retching over my toilet.

He deserves not the sweet that will not taste the sour.

Divorce Etiquette: Always use a clean white tourniquet.

Even a pig upon a spit has one consolation; things are sure to take a turn.

If life is a work in progress, then divorce is when the work stops. Or is it when the progress stops? Divorce certainly isn't when the pleasure starts.

Who seeks and will not take when once 'tis offered,
Shall never find it more.   **Anthony and Cleopatra**

If life is a series of lessons in learning and unlearning, I need to have a heart-to-heart with the Dean of Divorce University. I got thrown into courses that are out of my major and so time-consuming that they are delaying my graduation.

Who never climb'd, never fell.

Divorce 'R' Us.

We act differently. We play differently. Our lives are different. Why?

To mourn a mischief that is past and gone,
Is the next way to draw more mischief on.
Othello

Where is the common sense in divorce? The words spoken are base and common, but they make no sense.

Create in me a clean heart, O God, and put a new and right spirit within me.
Psalm 51:10

W̶hat does it mean to play for keeps? My divorce game arrived with an out-of-date rule book, and I think I've lost my marbles.

I thought I remembered all the old rules from childhood, but the new dice aren't nice and the cards are all stacked against me. The problem is, there are three grown-ups trying to play a game intended for two.

The world is a workshop and none but the wise know how to use the tools.

There is some comfort in knowing that all married couples are not happy, and all divorced couples are not miserable.

I need to focus on the good and remove the outtakes in life.

All worldly happiness consists in opinion.

Divorce has created a giant lagoon in front of my life. I'm at a standstill. I can't sail across it. I don't own a boat and the winds aren't right.

I need a giant pulley to drag me through the divorce sludge to the opposite shore. Where can I find a pulley I can trust? I've been jerked and pulled enough this year.

A slip of the foot may be soon recovered; but that of the tongue perhaps never.

Birds have nests, babies have bassinets, wine has casks, and I have a divorced brain cast. I cannot think or feel at home.

I feel homeless, loveless, listless, without any feelings of belonging. I only feel overwhelming aloneness.

Dry bread is better with love than a fat capon with fear.

You're welcome. Yes, thank you, for the thousands of loads of laundry, the tons of lugged groceries, and the triple-time-tap-dance of wife, mother, and career woman. All I ever wanted was your unfailing trust, loyalty, and love. What did I get?

All things are easy that are done willingly.

Is marriage based on trust, give or take a personal leave year or two? Is it alternate seven-year segments of a good ride, then I crash? Then is it a heartless, lifeless, house-less part-time-parent life?

Easy to keep the castle that was never besieged.

In life we have bulls, bears, and divorces with bull-droppings. We also have stocks, bonds, and market-droppings. The moral of this short story: IN DIVORCE, BUY HIGH BOOTS.

A good presence is a letter of recommendation.

W e have tried to reconcile our marriage three times. It's like trying to re-fry the same egg three times. You never get sunny side up again.

Once the eggshell is broken open, the heart of the egg is going askew no matter what. Maybe the trick is never crack open a situation you ever hope to get back together again.

Draw not your bow 'til your arrow is fixed.

February 13

My grip on the car steering wheel is so tight I have red marks on my hands. I must be overcompensating for all the divorced areas of my life that need re-gripping.

Maybe I can drop off my life at the local golf shop and they can re-grip my golf clubs, and my life, for a small fee.

Always put the saddle on the right horse.

I've thought about calling Home Depot. I want to depot my house. I want one room of happiness, one of joy, one giant room of laughter, one stadium-size room of hope for our son, and a tiny disposal for leftover divorce garbage.

I promise to keep the water running to make certain the disposal takes the garbage out of the house.

An idle youth, a needy age.

The competition for my mind's forum is relentless. In the first hours of the day, I have to be sad, be depressed, be angry, be fearful, be disappointed, and be distrustful. Then, in the remaining few minutes of my day, I am free to be spiritually me. Life is not a free-time hobby after the job of divorce.

I rejoice, because I have perfect confidence in you.   **II Corinthians 7:16**

Nature is tangible in the fruits and vegetables it produces. Nature is orderly in the flowers it grows. It is also our largest organized work force in pollination by the bees. Nature is logical in the timing and work of the seasons.

Why is human nature so intangible, out of order, disorganized, out of work, illogical, and ill-timed? Or maybe my divorce world is. . .

I will work on ordering my world by being productive a few minutes each day.

Every horse thinks his own pack heaviest.

WHAT IS THE CORRECT FORMULA?

OPTION 1: CHILDREN, HUSBAND, SELF, CAREER

OPTION 2: SELF, HUSBAND, CHILDREN, CAREER

OPTION 3: HUSBAND, CHILDREN, SELF, CAREER

OPTION 4: SELF-LOVE, HUSBAND, CHILDREN, JOB, MARRIAGE

OPTION 5: SPIRITUAL LIFE, SELF-LOVE, HUSBAND, CHILDREN, JOB, FAMILY

OPTION 6: A SELF-APPROPRIATED BALANCE OF ALL LIFE'S COMPONENTS

OPTION 7: THY WILL, MY WILL, SPIRITUAL LIFE

Enough's as good as a feast, to one that's not a beast.

I need to travel to the Hwange Game Reserve to meet with the lions, cheetahs, tigers, and elephants. The lions have perfected keeping their dens intact while co-existing with the other jungle members.

I need to learn techniques for rebuilding my divorced den while co-existing with outside predators.

Education begins a gentleman, conversation completes him.

During divorce, the weekends are deadly. My married friends all have plans. My divorced friends either have a with-kids weekend or an artificially empty-house-syndrome.

I've tried a few dinners with divorcées and kids. The kids play happily together, and the adults cry contentedly together. This is life?

. . . I am the Alpha and the Omega, the beginning and the end. To the thirsty I will give water without price from the fountain of the water of life. **Revelation 21:6**

THE CAT AND THE MOUSE: NOT ALL A FABLE

The cat was playing with a mouse,
Upon the grass before my house.
Over her little victim roll'd
Proud puss, in triumph; then took hold,
Gave her a grip, and let her go,
It might be p'raps a yard or so;
Watching the vain attempt to fly,
As with a tiger's fixed eye;
Til suddenly, and at a spring,
She pounc'd upon the trembling thing.
The mouse then turn'd upon the cat
(Who wonder'd what she would be at),
With sharpened nose, and eyes of fire,
In which were mingling, fear and ire,
And lifting up her little paw,

She thus began – "Pray by what law,
Treat you a fellow-creature thus?
I never wrong'd you, cruel puss!
My little ones are dear to me,
As your's, or any cat's can be,
Were some great dog to worry you
What would your pretty kittens do?"
The cat replied, "You reason well,
And what to answer I can't tell."
(But seeing the game was not unheeded
She hesitantly proceeded)
"Unless I be allowed to say,
That men do such things ev'ry day.
Indeed, it is a proverb quite
With all mankind that Might is Right."
Then giving mouse the stroke of grace
She ate her up before my face.

D. Griffiths

Speech is the gift of all, but thought of a few.

In my next un-divorced life, I'm going to laugh more and pray more. I have cried, mourned, bemoaned, and regretted enough life choices to fill this life's quota.

. . . he who sows sparingly will also reap sparingly, and he who sows bountifully will also reap bountifully. **II Corinthians 9:6**

Divorce donations gratefully received.

MOST-NEEDED ITEMS:
Family dinners for injured wife and kids
Baby-sitting service
Handy-man for neglected house
Errand Boy/Girl
Balm for the mental bruising
Daily ambulance assistance to get a broken heart to work

Give neither counsel nor salt til you are asked for it.

It takes four turns to keep spaghetti on a fork. The spaghett right length. The boxes are packaged to accommodate that m..

How many centuries did we eat spaghetti before we got the process right? Why did I possibly think I could get marriage right on the first try?

Divorce is the first three turns of my fork. A fulfilling post-divorce life is the final twist.

He is rich that is satisfied.

In Seattle, there is an official sound keeper who monitors Puget Sound. That's exactly what I need in my life: someone to monitor the foul sounds and garbage that come out of the newly divorced barge hogging my river.

Kindnesses, like grain, increase by sowing.

Divorce bragging rights are reserved for people on their second or third marriages. They're out of my league, into playing super-spit hard-ball. I won't attend tryouts.

He that will not be counselled cannot be helped.

Mother Superior cannot make a man into a husband, a male into a father, or a divine divorce on earth.

Neither can she give me self-forgiveness, self-confidence, nor spirituality. At birth, I was given all this and more.

Be slow of giving advice, ready to do a service.

My therapist says I should begin cleaning my closets. "Get rid of the anger of the past and make space for the eternal present and the future."

Every one should sweep before his own door.

What is divorce detox?

Is it actually talking with my EX instead of rage?

Is it awakening each morning with a thought other than divorce?

Is it laughing with my son and not crying at the same time?

Is it actualization of my future without quivering fear?

Has the pounding pain in my heart lessened?

I don't know yet.

The silence often of pure innocence
Prevails when speaking fails. **Winter's Tale**

What is my divorce self-maintenance program? If cars arrive with maintenance manuals, where is my lifetime maintenance plan book?

I need high-octane, anti-knock fuel with high performance to get through the first few hours of this day. I'll begin my plan book tomorrow after my head stops pounding.

I don't need a full rainbow every day.
A few good rays of color are enough.

I might move to Broken Bow, Nebraska, pop. 3,700. I could have a quiet life there. I want peace more than anything. Peace and quiet.

I need a year off from making life-shattering decisions. They have definitely been more shattering than life-producing.

Procrastination is the thief of time.

Each positive or negative divorce thought is a sentence in my book of life.

I will not re-read the negative.

I want every minute, moment, hour, day, week, and month to compile good years of life, not an ongoing nightmare.

My life counts now.

My motor is on.

My meter is running.

My good life is beginning.

Things hardly attained are longer retained.

I have discussed rebuilding my life with a dear friend. She softly replied with this French proverb:

"Cela ne va pas te tomber tout rôti dans la bouche."

"It will not fall already roasted in your mouth."

Many things grow in the garden that were never there.

This morning, I actually got out of bed feeling rested. I can't remember the last time I felt truly rested. Am I healing?

A handful of good life is better than a bushel of learning.

THE SPIDER – A HINT

King Robert Bruce, the restorer of the Scottish Monarchy, being out one day reconnoitering the enemy, remained at night in a barn belonging to a cottager, when lying down on the pillow of straw, he observed a spider climbing up a beam of the roof, the insect fell the second time; it made a third unsuccessful attempt; he beheld him twelve times baffled in his aim, but the thirteenth was crowned with success. The king started from his bed and said, "This insect has taught me perseverance; I will follow his example; I have been often defeated by my enemies. On one more fight hangs the independence of my country." In a few days his wishes were realized in the total defeat of Edward II, at the battle of Bannockburn.

Hold fast that which is good.   **I Thessalonians 5:21**

Today, I opened a new trust fund. I will intuitively trust my faith, myself, my life, and my decisions. I will provide growing interest for this fund, and it will flourish and pay dividends.

The abundance of money ruins youth.

Divorce is my personal, private pilgrimage. It isn't my neighborhood's divorce, my office's divorce, or my family tree's divorce.

My personal peace is my benediction. It is a growing faith that one day I will walk in my own purposeful, meaningful, empowered world, without walls. Each day's creation will supply my needs. No baggage needed.

All feet tread not in one shoe.

Blame. Whine. Blame. Whine. Blame, Blame, Blame. The music, dance, and mental rhythm of divorce nightmares have a familiar tone. The earlier I wake up and identify my healing process, the shorter the divorce rehab will be.

The first anger-free weekend trip I took with my son was a starting point. We had released enough hidden anger to peacefully coexist in the same orbit for 48 hours. We were beginning to heal.

AMEN.

Step after step the ladder is ascended.

During twentieth-century wars, we used bombs to distance ourselves from the realities of destruction. Strategic bombing in the early days was clumsy.

In divorce, we use middlemen and women called divorce lawyers or mediators to do the clumsy bombing work and save the specific acts of destruction for more personal battles to come.

The mill cannot grind with the water that is past.

Which sentences from our marriage vows didn't my EX remember? Maybe we should have studied our lines more carefully before the rehearsal dinner.

Wishes never can fill a sack.

Son: "Mom, when I get up in the morning, will Dad still be here?"

. . . the Lord sees not as man sees; man looks on the outward appearance, but the Lord looks on the heart. **I Samuel 16:7**

As a young child, I was taught to stay in a neat line at school. My Mom and Dad would say, "You'd better behave, stay in line, and do what you're told." This year's motto in my son's middle school is: "Dare to be Different. Dare to be Me."

Post-divorce behavior is a double dare when a mother and son dare to be a new family unit. As we strive to maintain our individualities, we'll keep the best of the past to add to the mix of the present.

Youth and white paper take any impression.

ALLIGATOR SOUP

Anecdotes of Profession – Buckland

Buckland, the distinguished geologist, one day gave a dinner, after dissecting a Mississippi alligator, having asked a good many of the most distinguished of his classes to dine with him. His house and all his establishment were in good style and taste. His guests congregated. The dinner table looked splendid, with glass, china, and plate, and the meal commenced with excellent soup.

"How do you like the soup?" asked the doctor, after having finished his own plate, addressing a famous gourmand of the day, "Very good indeed." answered the other; "turtle, is it not? I only ask because I do not find any green fat." The doctor shook his head. "I think it has somewhat of a musky taste," says another, "not unpleasant, but peculiar." "All alligators have," replied Buckland, "the cayman peculiarly so. The fellow I dissected this morning, and whom you have just been eating –" There was a general rout of guests. Every one turned pale. Half-a-dozen started up from the table. Two or three ran out of the room, and only those who had stout stomachs remained to the close of an excellent entertainment. "See what imagination is," said Buckland: If I told them it was turtle, or terrapin, or bird's nest soup, salt water amphibia, or the gluten of a fish from the maw of a sea-bird, they would have pronounced it excellent, and their digestion been none the worse. Such is prejudice." "But was it really an alligator?" asked a lady. "As good a calf's head as ever wore a coronet," answered Buckland.

c. Mid-1800s

The tongue talks at the head's cost.

Son: "Mommy, why did you and Daddy have to get divorced?"

You ask an elm tree for pears.

As soon as I get out of this divorce mess, I'm going to patent a new product called: "GET A NEW LIFE STARTER SET."

I'm having problems developing the prototype. The manufacturers say the pieces won't release from the presses, and the lids won't stay closed on the product packaging.

Sweet flowers are slow, and weeds make haste. **Richard II**

First tack, first nail, first toggle bolt, first screw, first floor, first day of new life. My new life begins a few minutes each day until a whole new first day, and then a whole new second day and life actually has hope in the forecast for a third day.

Too light winning makes the prize light.   **Tempest**

Divorced life is portion control from central commissary. I never get a full portion of happiness, or a full day of grief. I get bits and pieces of what I need, what I want, what I hope forever.

I can, however, set my own personal goals, or reset, I should say. I cannot seem to find the control buttons right now.

An oak is not felled with one blow.

Silent Night, Holy Night, just one good night. I would like one complete night's sleep. Does a full night's sleep mean complete healing?

He jests at scars who never felt a wound. **Romeo and Juliet**

I thought I would have less work to do after I finished the separation agreement. I have less paperwork, more mindwork, more balance work, and more Mom-work. All of it is homework.

There is nothing either good or bad, but thinking makes it so. **Hamlet**

Son: "Mom, how long does divorce last?"

Present fears
Are less than horrible imaginings.
Macbeth

Whater I was in West Sussex, U.K., I asked an 82-year-old widow, "How did you keep your marriage together?" She replied:

> We barely had time to keep the wax out of our ears, our kids clean and our bodies bathed. This generation worries too much. If we were on a pond, it wasn't to contemplate our reflections on the water. It was to quickly fish and get home with the catch to feed our hungry families. We worked together, struggled together, prayed together, and stayed put. No one doubted life would be hard. Married or divorced it's still going to be hard. Stop worrying and get on with it.

Still waters are the deepest.

Who are the Divorce Deadbeats?

Are they the ones who don't pay after the divorce, or the ones who didn't pay attention before the divorce?

How quickly Nature falls into revolt
When gold becomes her object.
Henry VI, Part II

I need to talk with my insurance man. He promised my policy had superior protection for fire, theft, and accidents in our house.

The policy provided replacement insurance for everything except "male head of household." He said the premiums were too high and it was too complicated to find a replacement.

Ask, and it will be given you; seek and you will find; knock and it will be opened. Or what man of you, if his son asks him for a loaf, will give him a stone?

Matthew 7:7-9

TRY

... What numbers of our best men and women could tell, if they choose, how they were buffeted in youth, how they were starved and neglected at home. They could tell of cottages from which they had been ousted, and money out of which they had been cheated; how often they had to begin the world afresh, and how often they had found themselves friendless and penniless. But they did not become grumblers and rebels; they did not sit down in sulky useless despondency, to make a catalogue of their wrongs and grievances. No: they forgave what they could, and forget the rest; they buried their grievances, and put them out of their sight; they looked before them for employment, and above them for guidance and help.

So they set to work, and built their nests again, with a heart lightened and invigorated by the very exertion they were making, and soon felt that, under God, the secret of each man's success is in himself, and that there is true wisdom in looking forwards, instead of wasting life in idle despondence over the past...

English c. 1849

Love all, trust a few,
Do wrong to none.
All's Well That Ends Well

Divorce Management 101:

Skills Required: Isolating anger, altering fear, organizing hurt, developing environmentally friendly EX relationships, growth regulation of internal scars and binding arbitration of long-range plans.

Experience: None.

Education: Not applicable

It is excellent
To have a giant's strength, but it is tyrannous
To use it like a giant.
Measure For Measure

In life, there is the expanded truth, the condensed truth, and the real truth. In divorce, there is a whole new category called borderline truth.

You are like a cuckoo, you have but one song.

I am sorry I am not the woman you want at this moment in your life. Most of all, I am sorry our son has witnessed and absorbed the death of our marriage.

Every man is the son of his own works.

If I put an infinite number of lawyers into a room with an infinite number of word processors, would I get better words on the pages of the divorce decree?

Divorce has little to do with the words on the printed page. Just ask all the judges, in all the courts, in all the world.

Every fool can find faults that a great many wise men can't remedy.

After divorce, how do I divvy up the photo story of our lives? Does my EX keep the photos and I get the negatives?

Now faith is the assurance of things hoped for, the conviction of things not seen.
Hebrews 11:1

Son: "Mom, what does it mean to be divorced?"

There is no accord where every man would be a lord.

April 4

Do divorce doctors use surgical staples, sutures, or live wires to repair a broken heart? After they use the pain-removing suction pump, there isn't much flesh left to repair.

No living man all things can.

When I opened our local paper, *The Divorce Times*, the "too late to classify" section fell out. It's a heavy section, filled with columns of divorces and post-divorces – too early to classify dead or alive.

You cackle often but never lay an egg.

If God is guiding my ship, why do I feel like a canoe out in the ocean? The sharks are circling and I'm shaking. I feel truly alone.

Maybe I should start getting out my oars and turning on the Coast Guard radio. Imagine that, the radio dispatcher said I have already been spotted and help is on the way: "Hang on. You can do it. We are aware of your needs. Your job is to stay calm for two minutes. Can you do that?"

I'm not sure. I will try. I will try to stay calm for the time required.

The absent are always at fault.

For more than thirty years, my father was an Agricultural Cooperative Extension Agent in the Ohio Valley. He walked the fields with 'his' farmers, prayed for rain in 'their' churches, and tried to keep ahead of the insects infesting the fields, fruit orchards, and kitchen gardens. In the farmland, the river of respect and trust ran deep.

We never locked our doors. Well, almost never. We did lock the front door (the back door didn't have a lock) when we went on six-week summer road trips. My parents were determined we should see America and their image of its Seven Wonders, a.k.a. Mount Vernon, The Grand Canyon, Carlsbad Caverns, the Petrified Forest, Mount Rushmore, Yellowstone Park and the wheat and corn fields of Iowa and Kansas. My father's film showed more slides of fields than people or places. He wanted to show 'his' Ohio farmers that their fields were up to snuff with the best of the west.

The destination of our road trip was grad school at Colorado State to bring home new agricultural research and 'farming' slides from the western states.

The Farm Bureau, Grange or Extension Office were his venues to pass on new knowledge.

His motto at 84 years old: Keep studying, keep learning, and pass it on. Take a walk every day, cultivate a little garden, believe in your family, treasure old friendships and trust in the Lord. Always know a few good jokes.

Knowledge is the food of the soul.
Wisdom is knowledge put in practice.

I'm angry all the time. I sound angry with the dry cleaner, the repairman, and the plumber. I can't get this anger out of my voice. It's there all the time. I need a spark plug, an emotion-replacement.

A light heart lives long. **Love's Labour Lost**

My EX's rules and regulations:

1. EX will foul the footpath.

2. What I want, my EX will go after.

3. My EX is always right. Divorce is not the time to break his record.

4. Don't mess with my EX's birthright. He was born perfect.

5. If the idea was originated by my EX it is THE PLAN. If not, it's dog meat.

6. No discussion. No adjustments. No returns.

Hasty climbers have sudden falls.

On the eight-lane highways of life, divorce hogs all eight. It is a wide vehicle with one driver, going one way, all the time. The affairs at the intersections take their toll.

Those who cry the loudest generally have the least to sell.

Divorced players do not provide a deep bench:

1. Their knees are weak.

2. Their eyes won't stay focused.

3. The defensive players are severely injured.

4. The offensive players have all gone home.

Too much feeding of the body starves the soul.

It probably doesn't take much arsenic to ruin a whole pitcher of iced tea. It also didn't take much divorce to poison my life. Both methods are silent and swift.

No one is a fool always; every one sometimes.

Son: "Mom, why does our house feel different since Dad left? Do you think our house feels sad?"

God hath often a great share in a little house.

It annoyed my EX that he didn't have the right reading light by his side of the bed. We went lamp shopping in four stores to find the right light for his bedtime reading.

He finally found a light that screwed into the wall and could be adjusted at different angles. Once it was installed, he said it still wasn't the right light, that it wasn't good for his eyes. The light didn't hit the book right and it glared into his eyes. It wasn't good enough. We even tried a lamp on the bedside table. That lighting wasn't right either.

Why wasn't I right for him? Was I a glaring light?

The good alone are happy whether young or old.

UNCLE BENJAMIN'S SERMON

Not many hours ago I heard Uncle Benjamin discussing this matter to his son, who was complaining of pressure. "Rely on it, Sammy," said the old man, as he leaned on his staff, with his gray locks flowing in the breeze of a May morning, "murmuring pays no bills. I have been an observer many times these fifty years, and I never saw a man helped out of a hole by cursing his horses. Be as quiet as you can, for nothing will grow under a moving harrow, and discontent harrows the mind. Matters are bad, I acknowledge, but no ulcer is better for being fingered. The more you groan the poorer you grow. Repining at losses is only putting pepper into a sore eye. Crops will fail in all soils, and we may be thankful that we have not famine. Besides, I always took notice that whenever I felt the rod pretty smartly, it was as much to say, 'here is something which you have got to learn.' Sammy, don't forget that your schooling is not over yet, though you have a wife and two children."

English c. 1855

True economy is something better than stinginess.

Divorce Daily Weather: Overcast, low visibility, annoying fog.

Weekly Forecast: Monsoon rains, gale winds, no chance of fun or sun.

Lifetime Forecast: Permanent low ceiling haze, pummeling hail, and unsettling earth tremors. All vacations and holidays canceled.

Call to me and I will answer you, and will tell you great and hidden things which you have not known.   **Jeremiah 33:3**

If I'm in divorce-crisis mode, and our house is in chaos, where is our son?

Small showers last long, but sudden storms are short. **Richard II**

During our divorce, our son completed an art project at school to reproduce his home. He built a two-story house with windows on every wall, a skylight, a tall, sturdy chimney, forest green exterior walls, a strong roof, and a solid foundation.

He forgot the front door. There weren't any doors to enter the house from front or back, or even from the sides. He said, "You don't really need to go in or out of our house. My home is there all the time."

The soul is man's higher nature.

One Sunday, I had lunch with an artist friend in West Sussex, England. Her paintings depict country houses, dogs, and farm animals in real or surreal settings. The tenor and tone of her paintings reflect her feelings clearly:

"During my entire painting career, I have never gone out to lunch on workdays because I cannot spare losing the day's light. I work from 8 a.m. until late afternoon because once the day's natural light is gone it's gone. On dark, rainy days I concentrate on form and little technical details, but not color. Color choices, hues, and balance are important. If I doubt a color, I paint over cellophane to test the red, or grey, or brown for the roof or object for that little patch. Then I peel off the cellophane and proceed with my decision."

What if I could try out my new life on cellophane and peel away the segments of the day that don't work or keep the colors that do?

Personally I am always ready to learn, although I do not always like being taught.
Churchill

Son: "Mom, I liked your cooking better when Daddy lived here. You don't make anything good anymore."

By cheerfulness, half the miseries of life might be assuaged.

Definition of divorce habitat: Unbearable, inhospitable conditions where two incompatible lovers once lived. The lights are out, the electricity is gone, the heat is off. The news delivered to the door is chilling.

To say little and perform much is the characteristic of a great mind.

A tough-skinned Southern lawyer told me: "Divorce is like the raging Ganges or the mighty Mississippi. Divorce rages without reason, is barren without heart and floods emotions at will. The 'gators are everywhere."

One touch of nature makes the whole world kin. **Troilus And Cressida**

Hmmm. Humma, Humma. Humm.

What else could possibly go wrong? Divorce has touched, crushed, and leveled every area of my life. I can only go up from here.

Therefore do not be anxious about tomorrow, for tomorrow will be anxious for itself. Let the day's own trouble be sufficient for the day. **Matthew 6:34**

"This is the ex-wife, speaking live from the end of the world. All color, vision, and meaning has been wiped off my landscape. It will take years to re-color my sky, re-grow my inner strength like the trees, and re-plant my life on this new patch of earth."

Deeds are fruits, words are but leaves.

How to Live

We live in deeds, not years; in thought, not breaths;

In feelings, not in figures on a dial.

We should count time by heart-throbs. He most lives

Who thinks most; feels the noblest; acts the best.

Bailey

When a friend asketh, there is no tomorrow.

A dear friend describes the situation: "Divorce is like a besieged city. Those trapped inside want out; those stuck outside want in."

Thou preparest a table before me in the presence of my enemies; thou anointest my head with oil, my cup overflows. Surely goodness and mercy shall follow me all the days of my life; and I shall dwell in the house of the Lord forever. **Psalm 23: 5-6**

My EX is not my paymaster.

My court date is not payday.

I am not the permanent payee.

I will pave my own way, you'll see.

.

The best surgeon is he who has been well hacked himself.

This year, which anniversary will make me cry the most?

June 5: The day we met. We always celebrated it. For twenty years, we always exchanged cards in honor of that day.

September 2: Our wedding anniversary. We celebrated it with a weekend of good times every year. We were married 21 years, 7 months, and 26 days.

August 26: Midnight, give or take a few minutes. The night my EX told me he had found the love he once shared with me in the early years. He didn't want to wait. He wanted a divorce now. He had found a new love.

April 28: The court date that dissolved our marriage. Two broken adult hearts, one broken child's heart, and one broken dog's heart. We were now officially split. The medics followed my car home to monitor my collapsed heart and erratic behavior.

. . a bruised reed he will not break, and a dimly burning wick he will not quench; he will faithfully bring forth justice. **Isaiah 42:3**

What do I do now that the divorce is over?

There is no relying on a starry sky.

Son: "Mom, does divorce mean you're going to get better or worse?"

In delay
We waste our lights in vain, like lamps by day.
Romeo and Juliet

Post-divorce life is self-made, not ready-made. Even a microwave can't cook this.

And God is able to provide you with every blessing in abundance, so that you may always have enough of everything and may provide in abundance for every good work. **II Corinthians 9:8**

Kind words do not cost much. They never blister the tongue or lips. They help one's own good nature. Soft words soften our own good-nature. Soft words soften our own soul. Angry words are fuel to the flame of wrath, and make it blaze more fiercely. Kind words make other people good-natured. Cold words freeze people, and hot words scorch them, and bitter words make them bitter, and wrathful words make them wrathful...There are vain words, and idle words, and hasty words, and spiteful words...Kind words also produce their own image on men's souls. They smooth, and quiet, and comfort the hearer. We have not yet begun to use kind words in such abundance as they ought to be used.

Pascal

Virtue is bold, and goodness never fearful.   **Measure for Measure**

I think homemade vegetable soup would be a soothing dinner tonight. I need something warm and comforting and filling. I have a big space to fill inside. I won't be able to fill it at once or keep it filled yet.

I'll make a big pot so I can give away several quarts.

They are as sick that surfeit with too much, as they that starve with nothing.
Merchant of Venice

The fresh air cleanses me. I breathe deeply on my thirty-minute walks.

The new air brings in new life from new nature replacing the old. I'll keep the new nature and willingly breathe out the old.

Take me upon your back, and you'll know what I weigh.

Most mornings the mist and fog filter layers of moisture over the sheep fields surrounding my little rented cottage in West Sussex, England. Every morning I drive my son to school, gazing at the black-faced ewes and rams and thinking how steady and close to the earth they live. Mist, fog, rain, or shine they forage for sorrel, clover, grass, buttercups, and tiny daisies. Every sheep, every shepherd, every farmer, every field has a purpose, and I am beginning to find mine on this earth.

We have to wait to the end of the day to see how great the day has been.

Sophocles

Whenfear creeps into my mind, I make a list with two columns. On one side I list my blessings and the other side my fears. My blessings always outdistance my fears in length, breadth, and duration.

I had rather do and not promise, than promise and not do. **Warwicke**

ENEMIES

Have you enemies? Go straight on, and mind them not. If they block up your path, walk around them, and do your duty regardless of their spite. A man who has no enemies is seldom good for anything: he is made of that kind of material which is so easily worked, that every one has a hand in it. A sterling character – one who thinks for himself, and speaks what he thinks – is always sure to have enemies. They are as necessary to him as fresh air; they keep him alive and active. A celebrated character, who was surrounded with enemies, used to remark – "They are sparks which, if you do not blow, will go out of themselves." Let this be your feeling while endeavoring to live down the scandal of those who are bitter against you. If you stop to dispute, you do but as they desire, and open the way for more abuse. Let the poor fellows talk; there will be a reaction if you perform but your duty, and hundreds who were once alienated from you will flock to you and acknowledge their error.   **Alexander's Messenger**

Tell me the company you keep, and I'll tell you what you are.

If, like bubblegum, I could stretch out a new life
right before my eyes, would the bubble burst before
I recognized the good in it?

It is goodness, not greatness, that will do thee good.

There is definitely hope I will get a good slice of life. The only catch is, after divorce, I have to bake an entirely new pie. How long is the baking time and the cooling-off period?

Winter finds out what summer lays up.

Careless words like "equitable divorce decree" mean that all the plugs and sockets in my future life may not be fully electrified.

I can only be assured of constant currency if I rewire and plug in my own life.

Wisdom is a good purchase, though we pay dear for it.

FUTILITY OF PRIDE

Alexander the Great, seeing Diogenes looking attentively at a large collection of human bones piled one upon another, asked the philosopher what he was looking for. "I am searching," said Diogenes, "for the bones of your father, but I cannot distinguish them from those of his slaves."

The honor of a maid is her name,
And no legacy is so rich as honesty.
All's Well That Ends Well

In the spring, our son planted pumpkin seeds. Eventually, eleven giant pumpkins grew. He carefully chose six special pumpkins to give to six special neighbors. Next year, he vowed, he would sell his pumpkins and start a business.

The next year, the woodchucks devastated his pumpkin patch and he felt sabotaged. When we say our prayers, he always says, "the best part of my day" and "the worst part of my day." He said, "The dead pumpkins are the worst. But Mom, Dad's moving out and leaving is the worst of the worst of all my days."

All happiness is in the mind.

When the hovercraft dropped me on the roof of the world, I had to accept the facts of divorced life:

Fact #1: The empty rooms in my newly divorced home. If I feel the emptiness, I alone am responsible to fill it, period.

Fact #2: If I sugar-coat my son's pain now, he will swallow bitter pills later. I must allow him to grow through, and work through his own pain.

In vain he craves advice that will not follow it.

How puny are the words about healing my son's divorce pain.

God comes at last when we think He is farthest off.

Mankind, from the Crusades to the Dark Ages to the Middle Ages (give or take a historical period or two) to the present, has noticeably improved its lifestyle.

Were my ancestors happier people than we are? I am working toward a happier lineage, fewer trappings, and more substance to my days.

The three things most difficult are — to keep a secret, to forget an injury, and to make good use of labour. **Chilo**

On weekends, I find bread baking therapeutic. Our son dissolves the yeast in warm water, adds a pinch of sugar, water and organic flour, and prepares the sponge. We let it rise twenty minutes.

Then we add salt, more water, more flour, and let it rise again. Finally, we take turns kneading it and deciding the shape or form of the loaves. Bread dough is patient and understanding. The measurements aren't exact whether it's summer or winter.

Some of our breads are great, some not so great, just like the days of our lives.

There would be no great, were there no little ones.

POWER OF THE PEOPLE

Much as a wise government may do, and it ought to do the very utmost that it can, there is no government, whether conservative, reforming, or radical, which can do the hundredth part of what the people can and must do for themselves, if they are to bear up against inevitable burdens, and recover permanent prosperity.

c. 1849

Every potter praises his own pot, and more if it be broken.

In my post-divorce life, I will not need a proofreader. I neither have to prove my life choices nor defend my position to anyone.

Let the words of my mouth and the meditation of my heart be acceptable in Thy sight, O Lord, my rock and redeemer. **Psalm 19:14**

My son's little ears, little voice, and little heart openly absorb the big noise of divorce.

The body is the socket of the soul.

Intuition is a spiritually powerful force. I depend on it as one of my strongest guides.

My world is not a random rain of hail. Events happen in order and with reason. I will find order in this divorce. The reasons for it are not yet clear, but someday I will know.

He who lies long in bed, his estate feels it.

When I tuck myself in at night, I rest assured that my divorce decree did not under-promise and over-deliver.

And do not seek what you are to eat and what you are to drink, nor be of anxious mind. For all the nations of the world seek these things; and your Father knows that you need them. Instead, seek his kingdom, and these things shall be yours as well. **Luke 12: 29-31**

I complained to my therapist that our son is moving on SLOW. It takes him forever to do his homework, light years to get a shower and dress, and leap years to do a few chores.

My therapist reminded me that my son's slowing down was his way of keeping his world the same. He didn't want the divorce, so he resisted change and tried to slow his internalization of it.

Again I saw that under the sun the race is not to the swift, nor the battle to the strong, nor bread to the wise, nor riches to the intelligent, nor favor to the men of skill; but time and chance happen to them all. **Ecclesiastes 9:11**

Son: "Mom, what are you giving Duchess (our dog)?"

Mom: "It's her heartworm pill."

Son: "Can people take them?"

Mom: "No, it keeps dogs' hearts healthy, not people's."

Son: "Mom, can my heart hurt and still be healthy? Since Dad left, sometimes my heart hurts, or maybe it's my chest, right here. Something doesn't feel right."

For the eyes of the Lord run to and fro throughout the whole earth, to show his might in behalf of those whose heart is blameless toward him.

II Chronicles 16:9

My Springer Spaniel is unfailingly loyal. She has been with us for eight years, after a three-year stint with another divorced couple who left her at PAWS, the Preventative Animal Welfare Society. I rescued "Duchess," as the original owners named her, but she rescued us with love, devotion, and compassion during this year's journey. She doesn't need to hear the details of good and down days; she is pure love for all days. She is unfailingly loyal to our son, who needs her love every day.

Each day we witness the creation of a new heaven and a new earth.

Thomas Paine

What are amulets for anxiety? How do I quell the quivering feeling? One of my recently divorced friends takes a bath at any hour – 4 a.m. or 6 p.m.

On Saturday night if she feels lonely, she starts painting a bedroom at 10:30 p.m. On such nights, she always takes a 4 a.m. bath after her painting is finished.

A quiet conscience sleeps in thunder.

W hat is the beginning, middle, and end of divorce? Is the end when the papers are signed in court, or is this really the beginning?

Behold, I am the Lord, the God of all flesh; is anything too hard for me?
Jeremiah 32:27

After divorce, just getting out of the house on weekends is a job. I have a million reasons to stay depressed and stay home.

I will get showered, get dressed, get out, and exercise my new life.

Good reasons must of force give place to better.   **Henry IV**

Divorce is so big, so out of control, and so utterly consuming that it requires complete physical and mental energy, thus leaving me with a wholly empty life.

Wholly empty until I fill life once again, bit by bit, memory by memory, good hour by good day, by good year, by God.

Does not the ear try words as the palate tastes food? Wisdom is with the aged, and understanding in length of days.   **Job 12: 11-12**

$\mathbb{W}$hether I like it or not, the clock is going to move forward, the divorce will end, our son will grow up, and some people's lives will go on.

If I stand still in life's traffic, I will get hit with mud, bruised by metal, and broken by oncoming heavy weights. I must move on from this spot to survive.

God, give me the strength to dodge the devils in my mind. Please, God, just get me through the next five minutes and I'll trust you with the rest of my life.

... Go your way; your faith has made you well.   **Mark 10:52**

I will never trivialize the agony and hard work I expended in writing my divorce papers. I will, however, continue to think that "divorce talk" will dog my future days if I allow it. I am finished with "divorce talk" and ready for "life talk."

Great talkers are like leaky pitchers, everything runs out of them.

POST-DIVORCE MENU

1st Course: Grilled Carp and Red Herrings
Main Course: Roasted Leg of Pascal Lamb
                Envious Greens
                Smoked Hardened Heart
                Sour Grapes
                Prematurely Aged Cheeses
                Sticky Buns
                Bread-less Pudding
Water: Old-Water-Over-the-Dam
Wine: Bottom-of-the-Barrel Wine
     Griping Grappa

The morning sun never lasts a day.

I was born with all the knowledge, skills, resources, intelligence, information, ability, love, and talent I will ever need in this life. My job is to release fear and tap into my own resource bank.

Divorce is a giant black cloud occluding my vision, feeding my fears, closing this bank. This divorce fear is not forever. This fear will stay present as temporarily or as permanently as the schedule in my mind permits. My agenda book was printed with blank pages, and I alone write the schedule of my mind. No one can or will do it for me.

I was born with all the God-given knowledge, skills, resources, intelligence, information, ability, love, and talent I will ever need in this life.

I say it with heartfelt promise several times a day.

Multitudes, multitudes, in the valley of decision! For the day of the Lord is near in the valley of decision! **Joel 3:14**

FORGIVENESS, A TURKISH PARABLE

Every man has two angels, one on his right shoulder and one on his left. When he does anything good, the angel on his right shoulder writes it down and seals it, because what is once well done, is done for ever. When he does evil, the angel upon his left shoulder marks it down, but does not seal it. He waits til midnight; if before that time the wearer bows down his head and exclaims, "Gracious Allah, I have sinned, forgive me." The angel rubs that out, but if not, at midnight he seals it; and the angel upon the right shoulder weeps.

The purest treasure mortal time affords
Is spotless reputation.   **Richard II**

Son: "I want a new pair of sneakers."

Mom: "I want to give them to you, but you haven't outgrown your current pair. We don't have money to buy anything we don't NEED NOW. We need to buy food."

Son: "I'm not hungry."

Mom: "Why do you need new sneakers?"

Son: "I know I can run faster if I have the right shoes. I know that's why all the other kids run faster."

Good harvests make men prodigal, bad ones provident.

My mother was the wisest woman I have ever known. She maintained her college weight throughout her 78 years by fasting on fresh lemon juice and water one day a week. Her life lessons included:

"Life is not a contest of how much we can eat. It is rather how little we can eat and be fully satisfied. Fill your mind and body with more than food. Be your own inner light. Never allow anyone to ignite or extinguish the glow of your candle. Pray fervently. God will give you more than you will ever need."

Remember that when you leave this earth, you can take with you nothing that you have received – only what you have given; a full heart enriched by honest service, love, sacrifice and courage. **St. Francis of Assissi**

Getting a divorce is work. Living with divorce is more work. Achieving a balanced divorced life is the most work, and the most worth it.

Of all the crafts, to be an honest man is the master-craft.

Divorce is not the Declaration of Independence. With a child, my EX's signature on our divorce decree means he feels he has the power to sign off on my future life as well.

I will set limits early on. My new career as CEO of After-Divorce Family Management, Inc., is a full-time second job. My new corporation has neither a Human Relations Department nor a Complaint Department. It's an appointment to Chairman of the Board without shareholders. It pays dividends at a much later date. Maybe.

It is more difficult to praise rightly than to blame.

Post-divorced life is a fresh chance at a balanced life. I have discussed it at length with a novelist in Sussex, England, and he replied:

> "Mental balance. Is it possible? And if it were, would it be desirable? Think only of Shakespeare. Some people are less unbalanced than others, but no one can continuously show a nice equality of debits and credits. Life is a high-wire performance. Those who manage to achieve an unsteady equilibrium are possibly those who are vividly aware that there is no safety net."

Do what you can with what you have, where you are.   **Theodore Roosevelt**

Son (sarcastically): "Mom, why are you so good to me? You never buy me anything anymore."

Mom: "Life is more than the stuff you own. You don't need that now."

Son: "How do you know what I need now?"

Every shadow has a light.

I have neither given up nor given in, and I am ready to re-begin. I feel satisfied after fully accomplishing a good day's work, when my desk is organized, and I'm prepared for my meetings tomorrow.

My focus at work and at home is much better now. The twenty minutes of meditation and prayer at 6:30 a.m. seem to center my day. When I oversleep and don't do it, I over-stretch, over-stress, and am out of focus. I drag through the entire day.

. . . whatever is true, whatever is honorable, whatever is just, whatever is pure, whatever is lovely, whatever is gracious, if there is any excellence, if there is anything worthy of praise, think about these things. **Philippians 4:8**

Son: "Mom, will you, Dad and I ever be a family again?"

As the morning steals upon the night,
Melting the darkness; so their rising senses
Begin to chase the ignorant fumes that mantle
Their clear reason. **The Tempest**

My therapist has earned her fees with me. I am stubborn, inflexible, and resistant to change, fearful of my future, and shattered by divorce this year.

I cry during most of the sessions. I believe what she is explaining to me. Yet, I find it so hard to hold onto her thoughts without daydreaming. Reaching for comfort, I say:

I have all the food, fuel, energy, money, finances, clothing, good health, patience, and spiritual guidance for this one day. I am safe. I am safe for one day. *I will be safe all day.* I say it many times throughout the days (and nights, if necessary).

The young lions suffer want and hunger; but those who seek the Lord lack no good thing. **Psalm 34:10**

I've analyzed my divorce enough now. I have cut my lawn with scissors, analyzing the grass blade by blade. It's time to mow over my remaining problems, level the landscape, and get on with life. My son is ready to move forward. I need to catch up NOW.

Waiting would be an unnecessary delay. All my energy is needed to create a better life. In some ways, our life is already better.

A wit and a fool in company, are like a crab and an oyster; the one watches 'til the other opens his mouth and then makes small work of him.

After the divorce, some of our friends remained loyal to my EX, some to me, and a few to both sides. What held the foundation together were the sensitive sensible neighbors. When I sold the house and moved, we missed our visits with 12-year-long good neighbors. We missed the block parties, the Halloween parties, the community feeling of well-being where each family wanted to participate. Young or old, together, we could share a cup of kitchen tea. We shared the land of one old Connecticut farm. The land was divided but the heart remained whole.

We moved away and were beginning again...

Greatness lies not in being strong, but in the right use of strength; and strength is not used rightly when it only serves to carry a man above his fellows for his own solitary glory. **c. 1867**

My life and my son's life are exactly, precisely that ... our lives ... our responsibilities. Only our own construction work will build a positive life and produce results. A solid inner structure, a solid life; we can make it on our own with good works and good faith.

The oak, that now spreadeth its branches toward the heavens, was once but an acorn in the bowels of the earth.

Does divorce make a botched life or a botched life make a divorce?

When you have lost money in the streets, every one is ready to help you look for it;
but when you have lost your character, every one leaves you to recover it as you can.

It is possible to stand on my scale until I lose two pounds. Or, I can get off the scale, adjust my eating and exercise until I lose it.

It is also possible to sit silently at my desk and be sad about my divorce or just get up and get on with life.

Of things one part is hastening into being; another, hastening out of being; and, even of that which is but quasi-existent, part is already non-existent. Flux and change are forever renewing the universe; just as the unbroken course of time makes the infinity of ages ever young. **Marcus Aurelius Antoninus**

Often our son says, "Mom, just be with me," (to read). Or, "Mom, play basketball with me," (or Ping Pong, etc.). BE WITH ME FOR LIFE. BE THERE FOR ME. DON'T EVER LEAVE ME LIKE DAD. WILL YOU BE WITH ME FOREVER, MOM? ALWAYS?

Listening is growing. Trusting is living. Trusting in God is life.

I am not a permanent road crew responsible for other people's potholes.

If you would relish your food, labor for it.
If you would enjoy your raiment, pay for it before you wear it.
If you would sleep soundly, take a clear conscience to bed with you.

I have to live the life, drive the roads, cry the pain, laugh the levity, feel the fear, sleep not the nights, disperse the despair, suffer with my son's pain, prioritize my purpose, deed my dreams to my journal, be alone with my loneliness, to fully dread the feelings of divorce enough to finally move on and make the necessary changes in my life. It's my job; take it or leave it.

To be satisfied with a little is the greatest wisdom, and he that increaseth his riches increaseth his cares; but a contented mind is a hidden treasure, and trouble findeth it not.

When our home was hurting with pre-divorce unhappiness, I bought a "guest book." We have used it four years (three pre-divorce years plus the year of the divorce). All the little children sign it after Halloween parties, birthday parties, or just a pizza dinner in our home. My son and I like to compare the comments and signatures of the kids as they grow up.

It is also inscribed after adult dinner parties and surprise birthday events. The memorable adult evenings are few and far between recently, but that is a goal I plan to change. My son and I are going to bring more life into this house. The guest book is going to date the happier days of our lives. We have many more pages of life to fill.

The best part of beauty is that which a picture cannot express.   **Bacon**

LIVE FOR SOMETHING

"Thousands of men," says Chalmers, "breathe, move, and live, pass off the stage of life, and are heard of no more – why? They do not partake of good in the world, and none were blessed by them; none could point to them as the means of their redemption; not a line they wrote, not a word they spake, could be recalled; and so they perished; their light went out in darkness and they were not remembered more than insects of yesterday. Will you thus live and die, O man immortal! Live for something. Do good, and leave behind you a monument of virtue."

One never loseth by doing a good turn.

The big boulders in the post-divorce obstacle course are time, money, and re-balancing the parent-child relationship. The stone wall, bigger than all the boulders, is hurdling the old marriage role onto the new half-family role. In time, a whole single-parent family.

The Pythagoreans had a wise saying, that a special care is to be had of two portions of our time – of the morning, to consider, and to resolve to do what ought to be done; and of the evening, to examine whether we have done what we ought.

Methods of Healing Divorce Wounds:

A. Pick at the divorce scab until it dries and scars.
B. Leave the wound alone until it heals itself.
C. Let the water, sun, and air naturally cleanse and heal it in due time.
D. Ignore the divorce wound and let it fester.
E. Consult a divorce doctor.
F. Allow the divorce wound to heal inside, strengthening the inner fibers of the mind and body until the hurt is replaced by healing thoughts, feelings, and purpose.

People never plot mischief when they are merry.

If I become sick, who will care for my son?
If I can't work, who will support my son?
If I'm in an accident, who will...?
What if I'm fired...?
What if my 84-year-old Dad requires constant care?
What if my son is in a serious accident?
Who will?
How will I?
I should have. . .
I know I could have. . .
If only I did it earlier. . .
I know I needed to. . .
Someday I will. . .
Conquering FEAR, piercing fear, is one of my goals.

Fear is an opinion.

I may have spent my youth, my heart, and my soul on a marriage fractured by divorce. I did divorce and divide, but my half of the settlement included my entire soul.

My half-a-heart will regenerate to a fully healthy state someday. Sooner than I might think. Stronger than I might expect.

Two gardeners, who were neighbors, had their crops of early peas killed by frost. One of them came to console with the other. "Ah!" cried he, "how unfortunate! Do you know, neighbor, I've done nothing but fret ever since. But, bless me! You seem to have a fine crop coming up; what sort are they?" "Why, those are what I sowed immediately after my loss."

My divorce is my emancipation. I was never enslaved in my marriage. I was a slave to my own ruts, rhythms, paths, and patterns of living.

Life is different now, better, buoyant. I am able to breathe once again. It's a good feeling to be on my own. I feel energized, my battery is surging, life is expanding.

The greatest truths are the simplest; the greatest men and women are sometimes so, too.

$\mathbb{A}$ French chef-proprietiere friend commented, "You'll be fine. You'll conquer your divorce problems. You'll see. Remember what I've told you about working in the kitchen.

"Anyone can master the mechanics of the cuisine, learning to sauté, braise, roast, and grill. Only when the heat of the kitchen is unbearable, tempers flare, and the real problems hit, are the great chefs born. The true test of greatness is how fast and effectively you get out of trouble. That's the making of a chef or a chief!"

He that likes a hot dinner, a warm welcome, new ideas, and old wine, will not often dine with the great.

Our son still wants me to read to him at night. I might have given it up by now, but the closeness often brings out his dreams and hurts. I listen carefully. His pain comes out in little phrases, little silent spaces and little sighs in his young voice. We hug often.

Some persons can be everywhere at home – others can sit musingly at home and be everywhere.

My son's routine of regular dinners, homework, bedtimes, quiet times, and journal time are all comforting times. This structure supports his wobbly new picture of life after divorce.

Hope is the prophet of youth – young eyes will always look forward.

From our son's journal:

"I feel as if three magnets who stuck together for a long time, got water poured on them and slowly drifted apart and never stopped to think what they had done."

Words of love lost.

My family is loving, but small and scattered. My closest relative lives 800 miles away. My son and I have had to depend on close friends for their support and help in our healing. These friends are both extended family and examples of healthy relationships for our son to see. We nurture and care for one another's children.

Whereas, those who are most prying into the lives of others, are most careless in reforming their own.

I have learned to repair most problems in the house, except electrical and plumbing. I watch to learn and watch to save costs. Learning to do repairs removes one more layer of divorce fear.

It is not what we earn, but what we save, that makes us rich.

Why did our home feel full and alive when we celebrated our baby's first steps and baby's first words? Why does our home feel empty and lifeless while the same young boy searches his Dad's closet for some trace of feeling left behind?

It is not what we eat, but what we digest, that makes us strong.

Our son wants to be like his Daddy. He is eleven, quite tall and big-footed. He only wants to wear his Dad's clothes regardless of how ill-fitting. He wants to be close to his Dad, inside his closet, inside his clothes or inside his head. Anything to be close to him, but his Dad has moved away.

Duke de Alba once replied to the king, who asked him whether he had seen the eclipse of the sun, that he had so much business to do upon earth, that he had no time to look up to heaven.

I believe God places guides and angels in my life. Several of my closest friends built a fortress around me when the divorce storm hit. My fair-weather friends quickly flew away to their own nests to winter in.

Early on, it became quite clear who would possess the stamina to help in the healing process. Some were even willing to allow me to heal at my own rate. It could take more than one year, but who is marking the calendar?

True wisdom is less presuming than folly; the wise man doubteth often, and changeth his mind; the fool is obstinate and doubteth not; he knoweth all things but his own ignorance.

LIVE FOR OTHERS

Believe an old man when he says there is a great pleasure in living for others... So, if you would be happy, shun selfishness; do a kindly deed for this one, speak a kindly word for another. He who is constantly giving pleasure, is constantly receiving it. The little river goes to the great ocean, and the more it gives, the faster it runs. Stop its flowing, and the hot sunshine would dry it up, til it would be but filthy mud, sending forth bad odours, and corrupting the fresh air of heaven. Keep your heart constantly travelling on errands of mercy – it has feet that never tire, hands that cannot be over-burdened, eyes that never sleep; freight its hands with blessings, direct its eyes – no matter how narrow your sphere – to the nearest object of suffering, and relieve it.   **English, c. 1857**

Wink at small injuries rather than avenge them. If to destroy a single bee, you throw down the hive, instead of one enemy you make a thousand.

When Sunday services were sacrosanct, and Sunday lunch a ritual, were marriages sure and solid? Now that attending Sunday services is spotty and Sunday family lunches are less "la mode," are the divorced families the unsure and the unsolidified?

In my world, a spiritual, religious life will live. My newly formed family will move solidly over the changing terrain, attending services and sometimes Sunday lunches.

He is the greatest whose strength carries up the most hearts by the attraction of his own.

Some parts of my post-divorce life will have to remain the same.

I can't smartly polish shoes that don't take a shine.

There is no policy like politeness.

Go to bed! Early and often. More sleep, more rested, more reasonable, more likely to accomplish my work in a shorter period of time.

Rested Mom = Reasonable Mom

Unrested, stressful, fearful, irritable Mom = Unreasonable Mom

Hath anyone wronged thee? Be bravely revenged. Slight it, and the work has begun; forgive it, and it is finished.

POST-DIVORCE PARENT-CHILD LIFE

ACT I:

Son: Mom, I wish you would get off my back.

Mom: I'm not on your back. I'm just talking.

Son: You talk too much.

Mom: What do you mean?

Son: You say more words than I want to hear.

Do not envy the merits of another, but improve thine own talents.

W hen I was concerned about my son, my brother, Jim, confirmed: "I cannot be a substitute father for your son. I can only be the best uncle and brother I know how. I will always be here for you. Remember, you are never alone."

Nothing is impossible to a willing mind.

Fully married, half married, half-past married.

Half divorced, fully divorced, half-past divorced.

Newly living, fully living, fully alive with life.

Heat not a furnace for your foe, so hot,
That it do singe yourself. **Henry VIII**

Son: "Mom, what are you reading?
Is it another one of your 'feel and heal' books?"

Healing is without an agenda.

I profoundly miss the comforting and reassuring conversations with my Mother. She passed away a few years ago. My brother and I always talk about missing her letters.

The last paragraph of every letter contained a golden nugget of memory from our childhood, a bit of philosophy of life, and an encouraging word why she was proud we were her children.

She wrote, "You don't have to become, or accomplish, or say anything to earn my love. I love the person you are today."

Wellness is a state of mind. My mind is well. My body is well. I am well.

There are three things that last forever: faith, hope, and love; but the greatest of them all is love. **I Corinthians 13:13**

I take life as it comes now. I let life go, let it evolve. Controlling life is like trying to harness the wind, or stop the rain, or schedule the sun to rise earlier or to set later. My natural rhythm is enough today.

Fire is the test of gold; adversity of strong men. **Seneca**

Divorce was a life cycle. I've rebuilt my bike and I am cycling new mountains, new plains and new territories. Being confident to ride is enough. Tomorrow will take care of itself.

Happiness is not having what you want, it's wanting what you have. **Unknown**

I cannot identify the beginning of my divorce but I can declare the end. Closure is feeling this year's emotions, living the consequences and consciously ending it. There are no remaining answers to the problems of my divorce. What remains is the satisfaction of declaring the end and going forward with a few strong strands to weave a new life in a spiritual light. With God's grace, I know I can do it!

... The Lord is the stronghold of my life; of whom shall I be afraid? **Psalm 27:1**

Do Not Procrastinate

There is no moment like the present; not only so, but moreover, there is no other moment at all; that is, no instant force and energy but in the present. The man who will not execute his resolutions when they are fresh, upon him can have no hope from them afterwards; they will be dissipated, or sunk in the slough of indolence.

English, c. 1857

In every country the sun riseth in the morning.

Epilogue

This book was written during a thirty-four-month period with the divorce decree in the center. During the final two months of editing, I was in bed with a fractured leg due to an in-line skating accident. I was confined to my manuscript, and thoughts of physical, emotional and spiritual healing.

Pulling the painful passages out of my mind onto paper was a strong exercise in healing. I have let it go. I don't carry around the hurt anymore. I am keeping the best parts of the past and consciously living in the present with my son's growing life.

Children have a limited past memory, an unlimited present, with little interest in the future. The unlimited present is the operative life. Making our mental images match the physical joy of a good hour, a good day, a good life, for all we chose to make it, for all we chose to give it.

I pray you are healing.

M. SUSAN HAMILTON
B.S., M.S., HUMAN ECOLOGY

But ask the beasts, and they will
    teach you;
the birds of the air, and they
    will tell you;
or the plants of the earth, and they
    will teach you;
and the fish of the sea will
    declare to you.
Who among all these does not
    know
that the hand of the Lord has
    done this?
In his hand is the life of every
    living thing
and the breath of all mankind.

Job 12:7-10

POSTSCRIPT: HEALING HINTS

- Discuss negative events once; no encores!

- Each day is an opportunity to continue hurting or healing.

- **Journals:** separate parents' and children's journals.

- **Pray together:** prayers of gratitude and release of fear.

- **Lifetime Plan Book:** Individual and family goals and dreams, short term and long term.

- **Flash cards:** Write positive statements of change, inspirational quotes.

- **Our Family Cookbook:** Develop new family recipes and include immediate and extended family recipes.

- **Living Family Album:** Take photos while visiting cousins and relatives near and far. Bring together extended family to heal broken feelings.